"Everything Is A Circle.
Like The Medicine Wheel. . .
A Teaching."

GRANDFATHER'S GOOD MEDICINE

Written by
Deborah Walley

And illustrated by
Tommy Thompson

THORNE SWIFT Wild PUBLICATIONS 1993

Based on stories created by
Deborah Walley and John Reynolds

Book Design by Ken Reynolds
Back Cover Photography by Nancy Powell

Printed by Griffin Printing, Penny Hancock
Sacramento, California USA

1st Edition
Published October 1993

 1993

Library Of Congress #93-079449
ISBN #09628329-6-0

 Printed On Recycled Paper

One Touch Of Nature

Makes The Whole

World Kin

William Shakespeare

GRANDFATHER

I first met Grandfather when I was seven, in the woods behind our house.

We lived in an isolated area, at the top of a great mountain. Actually it was a hill, but it seemed like a great mountain to me at the time.

We had no neighbors with children my age, and since I had no brothers or sisters, I spent much of my time playing alone. I didn't mind at all because in the woods behind our house there was a special world where I had many playmates. Chipmunks and squirrels, rabbits and birds, even frogs and field mice. They were all my friends.

Every day I would sneak biscuits from the pantry for them to eat. I gave them names and I pretended that they could talk to me.

One day, he was just there, sitting on a log, a very old man with long white hair that hung over his shoulders. His face was weathered and full of wrinkles, but it glowed like a child's. His twinkling eyes were deep brown, but when I looked again, they were as blue as the turquoise beads he wore around his neck.

He knew my name without even asking. And I knew he was magic, but I wasn't afraid. He said I could call him Grandfather if I liked, and I did.

For a long time, he was there every day, waiting for me whenever I came, and he taught me that the make-believe I played was not make-believe at all. Animals could talk if you knew how to listen, just as all things could.

Grandfather taught me how to soar through the sky like a bird just by closing my eyes.

He taught me how to feel the heartbeat of a tree, and to understand the songs the creek sang.

He taught me to hear stories in the wind and see pictures in the clouds.

He told me that the world people call reality is just a dream, and that the true world is inside us. And in that true world, he said, everything is one.

Many, many years have passed since I was seven. I don't see Grandfather anymore the way I did then, but he lives in my heart, and he still speaks to me.

Sometimes I hear him in silence, sometimes in the sound of the wind, or in the song of a mountain stream. Sometimes he speaks through the words of a stranger, sometimes through a friend. But I always recognize his voice, and feel his good medicine.

These stories are his.

PART
I

THE VISION

They didn't know where Grandfather had come from. They had hiked to the top of the hill, and suddenly, there he was. The girl saw him first. He was just sitting there, cross-legged, still as a statue. The two boys were sure a large rock had been there just a few minutes before. Now the rock was gone! But the three children were afraid for only a moment, for there was something about the old man that made fear vanish. And they were drawn to him like moths to a candle.

So they sat around the circle of stones that he had made, and watched silently, mesmerized, as he completed a cross of pebbles that divided the circle into four pie shapes.

All around them nature sang. There was magic in the air.

At last the old man spoke: "The Medicine wheel is the way of our people." His voice was soothing, hypnotic. It seemed to be a part of all the sounds that surrounded them. "It represents the understanding of the universe. It is a circle... a hoop, a mirror of ourselves. It is the knowledge that within the great hoop of life, we are all connected."

Above them, a red-tailed hawk cried out and swooped low, allowing one of its feathers to flutter down into Grandfather's hand.

The childrens' eyes grew wide with wonder.

Grandfather smiled. "A gift," he said. "Hawk is inviting us to fly with him. Today we will see things in a new way."

Then the old man paused. He stared for a while at the billowing white clouds that danced ever so slowly across the turquoise sky, merging and separating, changing from one shape into another.

The children watched and waited.

Time stood still.

At last he turned to the freckle-faced boy whose name was Andy, and he began to tell a story.

The boy became lost in the deep, brown pools that were Grandfather's eyes. Soon the words that the old one spoke drifted away on the wind, and all that Andy could hear was the rhythmic beating of his own heart.

Andy was not hearing the story, he was in the story.

"Rats!" he muttered under his breath as he lowered his rifle and watched the rabbit scurry away into the thicket.

Don't shoot off your toe! His brother's mocking laughter echoed in his memory.

I'll show him! thought Andy, *I'm going to kill something today if it's the last thing I do, and it won't be my toe!*

The mulching leaves on the forest floor crunched softly under his feet as he walked. He looked around intently. Not a sign of anything anywhere. Even the wind seemed to be in hiding.

A sudden shadow crept across the silent woods. From high up in a tall tree, Owl watched the boy with an amused look in his round eyes. "Who...whoooo," he whispered.

Andy stopped and listened, shivering.

Suddenly there was a rustling sound to his right. He whipped around to look. The dense scrub oak moved with a shudder and then became still. Then, just as suddenly, the sound came from his left, but, by the time Andy turned to look, everything was motionless. He tightened his grip on the rifle and moved forward.

Then he saw it. A blur of silver-grey streaking from one clump of brush to another. His heart pounded wildly as he shouldered the gun and waited for it to move again. Hours seem to pass, and his arm began to ache unbearably. Beads of sweat trickled down his freckled face. But not a leaf quivered. The forest was quiet and as still as a photograph.

At once, out of nowhere, it was upon him, lunging at him with a savage growl, gleaming white teeth bared! A wolf! With no time to aim, Andy fired, falling back and landing hard on the ground. The rifle flew from his hand and he rolled into a ball, fully expecting to feel the beast's teeth tearing into his flesh at any second. The short thirteen years of his life flashed before his tightly closed eyes in an instant.

"Did I frighten you?" a gentle voice said.

Andy uncurled himself slowly and looked up, too dumbfounded to answer. Towering above him was a man with long white hair. Andy couldn't make out his face, for the afternoon sun was directly behind the man, silhouetting him against the cloudless sky. "The wolf. What happened to the wolf?" the boy finally stammered, looking around.

"Wolf?" the old man questioned with a hint of a chuckle.

"It just attacked me... I shot at it and... and you had to have seen it, I, I thought you...

The man leaned in closer and held out a hand. "Here, let me help you."

"I don't need your help," Andy snapped, scrambling to his feet, "I'm just fine." Suddenly his ankle gave way beneath him and he stumbled in pain. "Oooo-ow, I think I broke my ankle." Before he could fall again, the man's strong arms were supporting him.

"Come on, I'll take a look at it," the stranger said as he guided Andy to a large water-worn rock. "Sit."

Andy felt helpless. He did as the man commanded, despite the eerie feeling that was mounting within him. He could clearly see the man's face now. He was old. His brown, weathered face was creased with rivulets of deep wrinkles, and his dark eyes were piercing. He reminded Andy of a picture in his history book of an Indian chief whose name he couldn't remember.

"You don't often see wolves around here," the old Indian commented in an offhanded

sort of way as he lifted Andy's foot and began to examine it, turning it gently.

Andy winced. "Ow! Hey, watch it, that hurts!"

"Not broken, just a sprain," said the old man, reaching into a beaded pouch that was tied to his belt.

"How do you know?"

Without answering, the old man took a small tin from the pouch and began opening it.

As he watched nervously, the boy quickly went on, "What are you, some kinda' witch doctor or something?"

"No, I'm just an old warrior," the mysterious Indian answered.

"I've never seen you around here before."

"I've seen you," the Indian replied, and his penetrating look sent a chill down Andy's spine. Then he rolled back the boy's sock and started to apply the odd-smelling contents of the tin to his ankle.

"Hey! What's that?" Andy quickly pulled his foot away.

"A salve I made. It will take away the pain," the old one explained.

Tentatively, Andy stuck his foot back out, allowing the Indian to massage the strange ointment onto his throbbing ankle. "How come I've never seen you if you've seen me?" he challenged, trying to suppress the eerie feeling that continued to build inside him.

The Indian looked at Andy and gave him a wry smile. "Maybe you weren't looking."

Andy shivered. He wished the old man wouldn't look at him that way. It was as if he could see right through him.

The Indian put the tin back in his pouch then looked at the boy again. "So, you are a great hunter, huh?"

"Yeah, I'm pretty good," Andy lied, "I've bagged me lots of rabbits and squirrels and little stuff. Never got me anything big like a wolf, though."

"Ah." The old man nodded. "And what do your four-legged brothers think of this?"

"Four-legged? What are you talking about?"

"The rabbits, the squirrels, the wolf you were just hunting. How do they see you?" the Indian answered with another question. "I wonder if you are a great hunter from their perspective."

"They're just dumb animals."

The old man shook his head sadly. "The truth is the four-leggeds are our brothers. The earth is our mother and all the creatures and the rivers and the trees and even the rocks are our relatives. That is why we must treat them with great respect. What happens to them, happens to us."

Andy crinkled his eyes questioningly. "Are you saying I'll be hunted like a wolf?"

"Who's to say that it is you who is hunting the wolf? Maybe he is hunting you," the Indian replied with a smile.

Andy felt that spine-chilling feeling run through him again and he glanced around fearfully.

The old man chuckled softly. "We all see things through different eyes, boy. The understanding of this truth is good medicine."

Suddenly a terrifying scream rang out from behind them. Andy jumped. "What was that?!"

"Mountain lion," the old man answered calmly.

"M-Mountain lion?" Andy exclaimed with panic in his voice. "Let's get outta' here!"

The Indian placed his hand firmly on Andy's shoulder. "No. Not yet," he said, and he moved in to settle next to the boy. "We cannot go until my medicine works for you. But until then I'll sit with you," he grinned broadly and put his arm around the boy. "You're lucky, I am filled with many stories."

Andy sighed deeply and rolled his eyes. *Great. Just great.*

The old man looked up at the sky as if he could read the words of the story there.

"Long time ago," he began, "when the white man was only a rumor and visions were sacred, there was a great and powerful mountain lion who roamed these hills. The lion was said to be invincible and held great medicine.

11

At the same time there was a man, a hunter like you. He was called Seeks-To-Hunt-Great, and, like you, he had little understanding of perspectives. He saw the cat only as a trophy, an ornament to wear to prove his greatness. He did not seek the cat's good medicine . . . he was after his hide!

All summer long he tracked him relentlessly, following the cat's every move. But the cat was smart and swift, always a step ahead of him, there one moment and gone the next. Try as he may, Seeks-To-Hunt-Great could never get close enough to take him. He was so blinded by his desire, he did not realize that the great cat had plans of his own. He did not recognize that he was not really the hunter. He was the hunted."

The hair on the back of his neck stood up, a shudder ran through his body. "Like... like me?" Andy stammered.

A gust of wind blew through the trees with a howl, then suddenly stopped.

The old man nodded. "Yes. Like you."

This was all too weird. Andy was beginning to think that he'd stepped into the twilight zone.

The Indian laughed as if he could read the boy's thoughts, and then he looked up at the sky again and went on with the story.

"It was a crisp morning in the early fall when Seeks-To-Hunt-Great finally spotted the cat at the edge of the great river, almost within range of his bow. The roar of the river was deafening and the determined hunter knew he could sneak up behind the animal without being heard. It was perfect. *This time he will be mine,* he thought as he made his way through the thick brush, chuckling to himself. How handsome he would look, wearing that hide! The head would make a fine hat and the rest a warm jacket. Everyone in the village would soon recognize him as the greatest hunter of them all! He drew an arrow from his quiver, one of the ones he had made especially for this moment. He readied his bow and crept in closer.

But suddenly the cat was not there! The astonished hunter looked this way and that. There was not a sign of him in any direction. Seconds ago the cat had been drinking thirstily, completely unaware of his presence. Now he had vanished!

Seeks-To-Hunt-Great moved quickly to the river's edge, hoping to find tracks, but the bank was lined with smooth rock, and there were none.

He was standing there, dumbfounded, when suddenly, from behind him came an ear-splitting scream. Seeks-To-Hunt-Great almost jumped out of his skin! He whipped around, slipped on the wet rocks and fell backward into the cold water.

When he sat up, the lion was standing on the bank, not ten feet away, looking at him with

an amused expression.

Brother Crow, who had been watching for some time, laughed so raucously that he almost fell out of the tree where he was perched.

Then, with a flip of his long tail, the satisfied cat turned smugly and bounded away.

Seeks-To-Hunt-Great was humiliated.

It was late afternoon by the time his thick, deer-skin clothes had dried. Even then they were damp and felt clammy and cold against his skin. Seeks-To-Hunt-Great climbed to the top of a large flat-topped boulder on a rise above the river and plotted his revenge. He was so consumed by his humiliation he didn't care anymore whether he killed the cat or not. All he wanted to do was get back at him!

A rustling sound drew his attention to the small clearing below him. It was the lion! He could hardly believe his luck! He flattened himself on the rock and watched with mounting excitement.

The cat walked around in circles until he found the perfect spot where the sun was warmest. There he lay down and closed his eyes.

The young Indian crawled to the edge of the boulder and crouched. The opportunity for revenge had come so easily, and it was sweet! He would scare the cat just as the cat had scared him!

Sometimes two-leggeds do such foolish things!

But, without a second thought, Seeks-To-Hunt-Great jumped, landing behind the cat, let-

15

ting out the most terrible scream he could muster.

The startled cat jerked, sprang to his feet and whirled around to face the intruder.

Seeks-To-Hunt-Great laughed uproariously, delighted at the cat's apparent fright.

The lion, however, did not think it so funny. Eyes flashing savagely, he laid back his ears and snarled. A snarl so ferocious, it made the dark-skinned man go pale.

It was only then that the realization hit him, a realization that for seconds paralyzed him. He had left his bow and quiver hanging on the limb of a tree to dry!

The cat crouched low, ready to pounce.

At last Seeks-To-Hunt-Great's legs got the message from his panicked brain and he ran. With fear propelling him, he ran faster than he had ever run before in his life.

But the angry cat was after him in an instant and soon overtook him, leaping onto his back and knocking him to the ground, growling and snarling viciously, tearing at his clothes and ripping into his skin with his sharp claws and teeth. Seeks-To-Hunt-Great struggled to get away but the powerful lion was too much for him.

He thought he was finished.

Then a strange thing happened. Like a house cat with a mouse that it is too full to eat, the lion batted at the man a few times, almost playfully, then turned and walked away.

Gasping for breath, afraid to move, the bruised and bleeding man watched, not knowing what the cat might do next.

The lion stopped and looked back, his eyes locking with the man's eyes. He was glaring at him with unmistakable reproach. Then, with a low, warning growl, he disappeared into the thicket.

Dark clouds swept across the sky, blotting out the sinking sun. A low, rolling peal of thunder rumbled in the distance.

Seeks-To-Hunt-Great was defeated.

The rain came down in torrents that night. Seeks-To-Hunt-Great took shelter in a shallow cave and treated his wounds with mud and the herbs that he had collected. The lion could have easily taken his life but had chosen not to. Why? He stared out at the downpour, and it was then that the vision came to him.

Out of the driving rain, in a globe of blinding light, the lion appeared, larger than life, no threat in his gleaming eyes, only wisdom. *Follow me and learn...* The cat spoke to his heart. *Know me so well that you can embrace me. Then, and only then, will you be great.* And the light became one with the man.

All night long Seeks-To-Hunt-Great played his flute and sang songs of prayer. He vowed to follow his vision.

The rain had stopped and the sun was just creeping over the horizon, painting the sky pink and gold, when he finally fell asleep. As he slept he dreamed of being given a new name, for he was no longer Seeks-To-Hunt-Great. He was He-Who-Seeks-Balance."

"Have you ever had a vision?" Andy asked.

"Yes," the old one answered.

"Could I have one?"

"Of course," the Indian said, a strange gleam in his eyes. "Maybe you are having one now." Andy smiled. *I'm in the twilight zone all right*, he thought. But somehow it didn't matter. "So, how's this guy gonna' make friends with a wild animal?"

"Very slowly," the old man laughed.

"He started off without a plan, not knowing how to begin or what direction to take. All he knew was that Great Spirit would guide him if he remained true. This was enough.

It was an unseasonably warm day. The sun shone brightly, adding brilliance to the scarlet and yellow of the trees. The air still held the scent of recent rains and all around him the birds sang joyful songs of praise. A gentle breeze blew softly against his face and played in his long black hair as he walked along, taking in the beauty of it all. He gave no thought as to where the lion might be or when he would see him again. His heart was light and his faith was strong.

After a time, he stopped at the edge of a winding creek and knelt down to drink. He had taken no more than a few thirsty gulps when he suddenly sensed another presence. He looked up slowly.

19

Directly across from him, on the other side of the creek was a skunk. He froze, holding his breath, hoping not to frighten the animal. The last thing he wanted on such a blessed day, or on any day for that matter, was to be sprayed by the pungent stench of a skunk!

The little creature studied the man curiously for a few seconds, then, feeling no threat, scurried away.

Seeks breathed a great sigh of relief and continued to drink. Having refreshed himself, he decided to follow the shallow creek to where it gorged deeply into the hills. The sun was now directly overhead and the steep, fern-covered embankments offered shade and a cool dampness that would be welcome.

He picked his way along lightly, treading carefully on the slippery, moss-covered rocks. It was not long before he was deep into the gorge. He rounded a bend and came to a sudden halt.

There, right before him, was the lion. He felt panic welling up inside him but he did not move. The cat took a few steps backwards. Seeks wanted to tell him that he meant him no harm.

He could think of only one way.

Never taking his eyes off the cat, he slowly drew his flute from its bag, raised it to his lips and began to play.

Not far away, the little skunk heard the flute too. *Ah, how lovely*, she thought. *I must find out what kind of bird sings so sweetly!* And she hurried off in the direction of the sound.

It did not take her long to reach the place on the embankment from which the song resonated. She waddled closer to the edge to find its source.

Seeks heard a kind of scratching sound above him. A few small pebbles and some trickles of dirt fell on his head and bounced lightly off his flute, but he dared not look. He and the lion stood like two great statues, their eyes locked.

Enchanted with the sound, little Sister Skunk had come too close to the edge of the high embankment and was trying desperately to keep herself from slipping. Suddenly, the ground beneath her gave way and down she went, spraying all the way.

The cat saw her coming and ran, but Seeks was not so quick."

Andy wrinkled his nose. "He got sprayed?"

"Sure did," the old one chuckled. "The stink on him only lasted a few days. Many moons would pass, however, before he met the lion again.

So he set up camp and built himself a shelter. Everyday, to no avail, he followed Great Spirit's guidance, hoping to have another encounter with the great cat, but he saw neither hide nor hair of him. He began to think that the lion might have vanished forever, and that the fulfillment of his vision was an impossibility.

The trees were bare now. The days were cold and the nights were freezing. Seeks longed for his family and the warm fire of his lodge. But, despite the doubt that sometimes plagued him, he would not give up his quest.

Old Man Winter would soon bring the snow. Seeks spent the next few weeks hunting. Although game was scarce, with Great Spirit's help, he was able to find some four-legged brothers who were willing to give him their warm coats and their meat to keep him from starving.

Still he was not prepared for what was to come.

It began early one fall morning with light flurries. Seeks looked up at the darkening sky. He knew that the lean-to he had called home for the past few moons would never withstand a major storm. He would have to find a better shelter, and he scolded himself for waiting this long. By the time he had gathered his things and started up the mountain, the snow was coming down hard and a fierce wind was blowing.

He searched for hours, making little headway. The snow was blinding and his feet were becoming numb with the frosty cold. It was only because he fell that he found it, a small hole in the side of the mountain! At least it would offer temporary shelter, so he crawled in. At once he found himself tumbling head over heels into a cave!

It was almost pitch black inside. Luckily, he had brought some wood with him, enough to start a fire. He would have to get more before the day's end, but first he would warm himself and get a bearing on his surroundings.

His fingers were stiff and he could hardly see what he was doing, but at last he found his fire stick and began rubbing it with another. He worked awkwardly, but soon a tiny flame leapt up. Seeks warmed his hands over the growing fire and looked around.

The cave was large with several alcoves at the back, still shrouded in blackness.

Then he saw them... a pair of glowing eyes staring at him from one of the deep recesses. He sucked in his breath as panic overtook him. But, as the fire's light gave further illumination, a smile slowly crossed his face.

The cave's silent tenant was none other than the lion! To escape the storm's fury, they had both stumbled into the same cave!

Great Spirit had rewarded his perseverance.

Then the cat let out a low threatening growl.

Seeks' smile quickly faded. He glanced out at the storm and then back at the cat and wondered if maybe the Great Spirit hadn't overdone it a little.

Just then the lion settled back. He was not happy about sharing his space with the annoying, flute-playing hunter, but it didn't look like the man was going to scare off. One thing he knew for sure, he was not going to give up this cave to a two-legged and go searching for another in this weather. He decided to just keep an eye on him.

All afternoon he watched, as Seeks went in and out of the cave, bringing in load after load of wood. The small fire was kept burning, and the cave was warm and cozy. *Maybe this won't be so bad after all*, thought the cat, but he wasn't sure and he kept alert.

23

By evening the storm outside was raging like a wild beast. Seeks had stockpiled enough wood to last for several days. He took off his wet furs, threw a couple of stout branches on the fire and made himself comfortable. Now he was hungry!

He looked over at the cat who lay crouched in an alcove as far away from him as possible. Surely they had hunger in common. Maybe food was the way to the cat's heart! He reached in his pouch and took out a large piece of jerky. Tearing a portion off, he tossed it over to the lion.

The surprised cat sniffed at it suspiciously. He looked at the man, then pushed the jerky away with his nose. He may have to share his space with him, but there was no way he was going to take his offering!

Seeks was tired. He sang his prayers and quickly fell asleep. The cat tried to stay awake but the warmth and hypnotic glow of the fire lulled him, and finally he fell asleep too.

They awoke to a terrible rumbling sound. The cat was first on his feet and he screamed in fear. The rumbling became earthshaking. They both knew there was no escape. Within seconds an avalanche sealed the cave's entrance with a barricade of ice and snow."

Andy was sitting on the edge of his seat. "You mean they're trapped in there?"

The old man nodded. "All day long Seeks dug at the entrance, getting nowhere. The icy wall was thick and frozen solid.

Days passed. How many? They had no way of knowing. All sense of time was lost. Days and nights were all the same. Their world was the smoky cave and the tiny fire that kept them from freezing. Seeks had managed to poke a small hole in the barrier with his bow, and he spent every waking hour working, scraping and poking, to make it bigger. Still it was not big enough for them to get through.

Seeks shared his last piece of jerky with the cat. This time the cat ate it thankfully.

More time passed and the hole in the barrier was not getting much bigger. In his dreams, Seeks prayed to Father Sun to melt the wall of ice that imprisoned them. But each time he woke it was still there.

Seeks and the cat were both becoming weak from hunger. The wood was almost gone. They both wondered the same thing. If they didn't get out of that cave soon, who would eat who?

It was just about that time that they heard the wolves howling loudly in the distance. Sealed as they were in their icy tomb, they paid the howling little mind. Moments later, however, when a fat rabbit popped in through the hole, their attention was captured. Then came the wolves, yipping and yelping, scratching and clawing, digging at the barrier, reaching in with their mammoth paws.

Seeks drew his bow and readied to shoot should one of them break through. The lion snarled. Then there was another howl in the distance, and they were gone as quickly as they had come.

Maybe it was the sound and the scent of the lion, maybe the man, maybe they simply spotted easier prey. Whatever made them leave, it didn't matter. All that mattered now was the rabbit, who still stood at the entrance, paralyzed with fear. Seeks let his arrow fly.

They feasted well that night.

As it turned out, the wolves had blessed them with more than just a rabbit dinner. Their digging had weakened the wall, and by the next day, Seeks was able to break through. They were free at last!

Seeks made up a special song for the wolves and the rabbit, thanking them for saving their lives. He sang it loud from the side of the mountain and hoped that they would hear."

"But what about the lion? Now that they were free, did he run away?" Andy wanted to know. "Is Seeks going to be able to fulfill his vision?"

"I'm getting to that," the old one said, patting the boy on the knee. "The lion didn't run away because he no longer felt threatened. He had grown to respect Seeks, just as Seeks had grown to respect him. Now they shared the vision."

"So they stayed together?"

"Sure! It was a good cave, warm in the winter, cool in the summer, plenty of room for both of them. Besides, the cat was no dummy. He knew that two hunters are better than one! In those days there were no grocery stores, hunting was part of survival." Then the old man slapped his leg and laughed uproariously. "The first time the two of them went hunting together was almost the last time! They were chasing a deer and they ran right into a bear! A big grizzly, probably ten feet tall when he raised up, which is exactly what he did when they ran into him. The roar he let out was so ferocious and so loud, it sent creatures scurrying to hide for miles around!"

"What did they do?" Andy asked anxiously.

"They ran!" the old man laughed. "They ran like a couple of arrows just released from the bow! But the bear was fast too, they could feel his breath on their backsides, they could hear his huge paws hitting the earth as he chased them! Finally he chased them up a tree. And that bear kept roaring and shaking that tree till long past sun-down. Seeks and the cat had to spend the night there. The next day they went fishing."

Andy laughed, but quickly turned serious again. "But in order to fulfill his vision Seeks needs to embrace the lion, right? Does he do that?"

"Trust comes with time," the old man answered. "Seeks and the cat were on the path of friendship, yes, but the cat was still leery and every time Seeks tried to touch him he shrank back. Seeks decided he would stop trying and wait for the cat to come to him. This was a good decision. And once he stopped trying, he didn't have long to wait."

"It was during the Moon of The Grass Appearing. The snow had melted and the hills were clothed in green and dotted with the delicate colors of the first wildflowers. Against the azure sky, huge white clouds peered over the mountain tops with a promise of afternoon rain. It was a perfect day, and all of nature, from the tiniest flower to the tallest tree, seemed to be celebrating rebirth.

In the big meadow at the base of the mountains, like a boy and a puppy, Seeks and the cat were playing chase. It was a favorite game of theirs. First Seeks would chase the cat, then the cat would chase Seeks. Round and round, and back and forth they would go, neither ever catching the other. Finally, exhausted and laughing, Seeks collapsed onto the carpet of sweet-smelling grass.

Across the meadow, the lion watched him. Seeks could feel the cat's eyes on him without even looking. He propped himself up on his elbows and called, "Come over here, wild one, the grass is sweeter on my side of the meadow!"

The lion twitched his ears and crouched down low. Then suddenly, he jumped to his feet, sprang forward, and charged across the meadow like a raging bull!

Seeks quickly sat up as a sudden bolt of terror struck him.

Five feet away from him, the lion stopped and rolled over, finally resting his head on his paws, looking up at Seeks playfully. A lone wild iris, swaying in the warm breeze, tickled his nose and he sneezed.

29

Seeks laughed, and the terror drained away as quickly as it had come. "I don't want to play, wild one, I'm tired. Come rest with me." He patted the ground next to him.

The lion shook his head.

"Don't worry," Seeks said softly, "I won't touch you."

The great cat stared at the man who had become his friend. He stared for a long time, and his soft brown eyes spoke.

And the man understood. And the love he felt was far greater than his vision. "It is good," he said. And it was.

Seeks had learned the ultimate surrender. He now knew it was the journey, not the goal, that held the greatest gift, and it was his friend, the lion, who had taught him. Seeks turned his his face to the sky and sang to Great Spirit in thanks. The sounds he sang came from deep within him, for there were no words.

He was still singing when the cat rose to his feet. His song caught in his throat and his voice trailed off.

The lion began moving towards him, slowly, one step, and then another. Closer and closer he came, until he was just inches away. Seeks could feel the cat's warm breath on his face. He breathed and their breath became one. And in the depth of the lion's eyes, Seeks saw himself. Then the cat laid a paw on Seeks' leg and purred. The moment had come. Seeks reached out his arms to embrace him.

Suddenly, like thunder, a sharp crack rang out and the cat fell into his lap. Seeks looked around in stunned bewilderment and then back at the cat. The cat twitched a few times, heaved a final sigh, and then was still. There was a bloody hole in his side but there was no arrow. Seeks touched it with his fingers. His mind spun in confusion.

He looked around again, and then he saw him... a man, standing on the side of the mountain, a smoking stick in his hand... a strange man like none he had seen before... white skinned with yellow hair. Seeks stared in awe. Then the man raised his hand in peace. And all at once Seeks knew it was this man who had somehow killed his friend, but he did not understand.

He looked down at the still lion lying across his lap, his beloved friend. He stroked the cat's head and buried his face in his warm fur. And he cried. He cried as he hadn't done since he was a small child. And then he stood up and he threw his head back to face the sky.

His anguished scream echoed through the canyons. And the wolves answered, howling mournfully."

Andy sat in stunned silence for a while, unable to find his voice. Finally it came. "The white man... he thought he was saving the Indian's life, didn't he?"

The old man nodded solemnly. "It was all a matter of perspective."

Andy shook his head and sighed. "If only he had taken the time to see... to understand."

"Yes," the old one nodded again, "but he didn't. It is sad, most people don't."

"I will," said Andy.

"Good," said the old man, patting the boy gently on the back.

Andy thought for a moment and then sighed. "It's kinda' like history, isn't it? I mean, if the white men who first came here had taken the time to see things from the Indian's perspective, they would have learned so much."

"Yes," the old man smiled, "but remember it is not so important how things were seen then. The past is just to teach us. What's really important is how we see things now. So, how's your ankle?"

The boy had almost forgotten. He stood up and put some weight on it. "It's... it's fine!" he said in surprise. "What is that stuff you put on it?"

The old one winked then raised his eyebrows. "Wolf medicine."

"Wolf medicine. Right." The boy chuckled.

The old man stood up. "Well, I've got to be going."

"Yeah, me too," Andy said, glancing at the sun slowly disappearing behind the mountains. "It was nice talkin' to you, Mister. Thanks. Thanks a lot."

The old man extended his gnarled hand. Andy took it and they shook. "Walk in balance, boy," he said, and he walked away.

Andy watched him as he climbed the rocky knoll. At the crest of the knoll the old man stopped and turned back, giving the sign of peace.

Andy started to raise his hand to return it. But, suddenly, he froze in shock. His breath caught in his throat, it felt like his heart stopped beating, the blood seemed to drain from his body...

It was not the old man who now stood at the top of the knoll. It was the wolf.

PART
II

RABBIT GIRL AND THE THREE-LEGGED FOX

Grandfather twirled the hawk feather around in his fingers, his eyes still fixed on the freckled-faced boy. "Each of us sees from a different perspective depending on where we are sitting on the Medicine Wheel," he said softly. "What looks one way to you, looks another way to me. Still we are brothers and sisters. We are one." He shifted his gaze to the frail-looking girl with golden hair who sat across from him. "We are all a part of the Earth, our mother, and she is part of us. We must be warriors against the enemy that tries to separate us."

"Who is the enemy?" the girl asked, a tremor in her voice.

"Fear," Grandfather said. "Our only enemy is fear."

The girl was sure she saw the old man's eyes change from brown to turquoise and back again. Her head began to spin. She didn't feel sick, she felt like she was falling backwards in slow motion, and she couldn't stop herself. Floating down through swirling colors, she was falling, further and further away. She thought she heard her name, but Grandfather's voice was fading. It was so distant she could barely hear it, and at last, it was completely drowned out by the sound of a running motor.

Courtney was huddled in the back seat of the station wagon, staring out at the passing scenery. Her little mop of a dog, Rags, hung his head out of the window, wagging his tail eagerly.

Courtney did not share his enthusiasm. The mountains looked so foreboding. She had not seen a house, or a building, or a store, in what seemed like hours, just vast expanses of forest that looked ready to swallow them up.

Her father sang loudly as he maneuvered the endless curves in the road, steering with one hand and holding a diet soda in the other. *"I'm happy when I'm hiking beyond the narrow trail... I'm happy when I'm hi-king, da, da, dee, da, de, daaaa!"* He was not only loud, he was off key.

Next to him, her mother was working, as usual, finishing up some business she didn't have time to get to before they left. The tap, tap, tapping of the laptop computer kept an irritating beat with the rhythm of the song.

Courtney caught sight of a large yellow road sign. WATCH OUT FOR ANIMALS NEXT 40 MILES. She gave a little shudder. "Daddy?"

"Yeah, Court?"

"Will there be any wild animals?"

"What's that, honey?" Her father never seemed to answer a question the first time she asked. But, at least he'd stopped singing.

"Your daughter wants to know if there will be any wild animals," her mother interjected, shooting him an annoyed look.

"Oh, sure!" her father answered brightly. "In fact, we have to be very careful not to leave any food around or we could be attacked by bears. Those things can crush a car like an aluminum can!" To emphasize the point, he crushed the diet soda can in his hand.

Courtney cringed. "What about lions... and snakes?"

"Lions and snakes? Hmm..." Her father thought for a moment, which in itself was rather discomforting. "Well, I don't think we have to worry about mountain lions," he finally answered, "I'm almost sure they're extinct, and snakes only come out at night."

Great! They were heading into the wilderness with a man who thought snakes only came out at night! Even she knew better than that!

"But we will have to watch out for bugs," he went on. "You know, spiders, centipedes, scorpions..."

"I'm afraid of bugs, Daddy," Courtney whined.

"See, now you've gone and scared her," her mother snapped, and then looked around the seat at her, comfortingly. "Don't worry, baby, mommy brought enough bug spray to annihilate an entire population of creepy crawlies." She turned back to give her husband an icy glare: "And anything else annoying." Then she went back to her incessant tapping.

"I hope you didn't get the aerosol kind," her father snapped back, "there's a hole in the ozone layer, you know."

"If you're so concerned with the ozone, Mister Environment, why don't you turn off the air conditioner? Then we can all die of heat prostration before we get skin cancer!" Her mom had that sarcastic tone to her voice she always used right before they really got into a battle.

Courtney hated it when they fought. She stuck her fingers in her ears and thought about what it would be like to die of heat prostration. But, except for the tapping of the laptop, it was all quiet up front. She removed her fingers. They were giving each other the old silent treatment.

Finally, her father broke the silence. "Beverly," he said in that sugary sweet voice he always used to cover his anger, "I really wish you would put the computer away. We are on vacation."

"Hawaii is a vacation, Bruce," she retorted just as sweetly, "camping is a nightmare."

Courtney had to agree there!

"Forgive me for saying so, but the closest thing to a camping experience you've ever had is shopping at Camp Beverly Hills. Don't be so quick to judge what you haven't tried." Her dad smiled that we'll-talk-about-it-later smile he was so good at. "I'm telling you, Bev, we're going to have a happy family vacation whether you like it or not!"

Her mom smiled back. "Whatever you say, dear," she said, honey dripping from every word. "But I just know something terrible is going to happen."

Just then there was a loud bang and the car began to wobble and swerve.

Bruce slapped the steering wheel angrily. "A blow out!"

"Bingo!" Beverly smiled.

Her father pulled the car over to the side of the road. "A blowout is not something terri-

41

ble, Beverly," he said, getting out and slamming the door, "it's just inconvenient. I'll have it fixed in a minute. Why don't you girls go take a powder."

Beverly made a face at him. "I'm not going anywhere where I can't flush!" she muttered under her breath. Then, with an irritated sigh, she got out and opened the door for Courtney. "Courtney, why don't you see if Rags has to go."

Rags was already out of the car, looking up at her with a plea in his soulful, brown eyes, wagging his tail furiously.

"Okay, okay, Rags. Let's go." She got out reluctantly and walked him over to a clump of trees.

Rags began sniffing from tree to tree, unable to make up his mind which one to go on. *So many choices*, he thought. *This is heaven!*

Courtney glanced over her shoulder at her parents. Her dad was busily getting tools out of the back of the car. She could tell that he was swearing. Probably couldn't find what he needed what with the ba-zillion dollars worth of new camping gear he had jammed in there. Her mother had the laptop set up on the hood and was already back at work. It didn't matter where they were or what the circumstances, her mom always worked, and when she wasn't working, she worried. She was probably the most concerned accountant in the entire universe.

Courtney looked around. "Hurry up, Rags, it's scary here!"

Rag's attention was elsewhere. He stood alert, sniffing the air, his little body quivering with excitement. He didn't think it was scary. He thought it was wonderful! Suddenly, without so much as a backwards glance, he took off into the woods as fast as his four short legs could carry him, yipping wildly.

"Rags! Where are you going?! Come back here!" she called in panic.

But Rags had picked up the scent of a rabbit, and, since he had never chased one in his life, he wasn't about to miss the opportunity now.

Courtney cast a desperate look back at her parents. They were oblivious. Her dad had the car radio blasting and was singing along with it at the top of his voice. Her mother was yelling at him to stop, calling him a frustrated lounge lizard, as she so often did. Courtney didn't have time to explain. "Rags!" she screamed, and took off after him. "Rags!"

The forest was dense. Strange sounds surrounded her. Rags was nowhere to be seen.

Something screamed from high overhead. She looked up. The trees spiraled above her. She reeled in fear. The terrible thing that screamed from the sky would probably swoop down and carry her off and... Then she heard Rags barking and she snapped back. "Rags! Rags!"

Further and further into the forest she went without ever catching sight of him.

Finally, at the edge of a steep ravine, she stopped. Before her, the vast tree-covered wilderness stretched out like an enormous humpbacked beast

who lay asleep. She was standing on the lip of its gaping mouth. What if it was to wake? "Rags!" she screamed again. "Rags, Rags, Rags," her voice echoed back. Salty tears stung her cheeks. Her mother was right. Something terrible had happened. The beast had swallowed her dog, and there was nothing she could do about it.

Facing life without Rags seemed impossible. He was her best friend! She thought about how he snuggled into a warm ball next to her in bed at night, his little head on her pillow... how he licked her tears away when she cried... how he sat in her lap and watched cartoons with her every Saturday morning and wagged his tail when she laughed... how cute he looked when he sat back on his haunches to beg for food... how he growled at Daddy every time he got mad at her. Her heart was so heavy that, for a while, she forgot about her fear. She turned and started back to the car.

Then suddenly it gripped her, tightening its icy fingers around her throat, choking her. Where was the car? Where was the road? Where were her parents?!

She whirled around, looking in all directions, her heart beating wildly. She had to get a hold of herself. She had to figure out which way she had come! But fear was squeezing the breath out of her and she couldn't think. Then, the terrible thing screamed out again from above, and she ran. She didn't know, that like Alice through the looking glass, she was running into another dimension.

The trees came alive and reached their twisted arms out to grab her. Thorny bushes scratched at her viciously and ripped at her clothes. Giant spiders tried to snare her in their webs. And behind her, she could hear the flapping of the terrible thing's huge wings.

In sheer panic she ran, her eyes blinded by tears. And she didn't stop running until, at the edge of a small clearing, she stumbled over a log and fell. She could go no further anyway. She rolled herself into a tight little ball and sobbed hysterically.

She cried until there were no more tears, and her sobs were reduced to a few pitiful heaves and gasps. At last, she could hear the flute.

She looked up and her eyes grew wide.

Across the clearing, not twenty feet away, an old Indian man sat playing a bird-shaped flute, and he was looking straight at her! He lowered the flute and nodded with a knowing smile. "Lost, huh?"

Courtney nodded fearfully. Her mother's words rang through her head. *Never talk to strangers! Courtney, the world is filled with bad men who are just waiting to do horrible things to you!*

"You didn't hear me before because fear has blinded your eyes and deafened your ears," the old man continued. "I had to play my flute very loud."

Then the terrible thing screamed. Courtney looked up in terror.

A hawk sailed down from the sky and glided over the clearing in a lazy circle.

"Hawk is my helper," the old man said, acknowledging the bird with a nod. "He has been calling and calling to you."

Courtney wanted to get up and run but she couldn't. She wanted to scream but she had no voice.

"So, what is lost is found!" said the old Indian cheerfully. "It is a circle." Then he gestured to her warmly. "Come here."

Courtney hugged herself tighter and shook her head.

"Come on," he patted a place next to him on the robe on which he was sitting. "You are among friends."

Just then, Courtney heard a rustling sound behind her and the snapping of twigs. She whipped around to look.

Heading right for her was a big, black bear!

She screamed, jumped to her feet and tore across the clearing crying, "Put your food away! Put your food away! It'll crush your car like an aluminum can!" And she leapt into the old man's arms and buried her face in his chest. She didn't care what horrible things he might do to her, nothing could be worse than being eaten by a bear!

The old man gently stroked her hair. "It is good to feel your fear, little one," he said softly, "but you must face it like a warrior, then it will pass through you."

"But, there, there's a bear coming!" Courtney cried, looking up at him. Was he blind, didn't he see it?

The old man just smiled and nodded. "Oh, good," he said, "I was expecting him." Then, he called out to the bear as if it was a person, "It's all right, Brother Bear, come on." He gave Courtney a comforting little hug. "We meet here often to exchange stories," he told her in a confidential tone.

Courtney scooched in as close as she could to the old man and watched in amazement as the bear walked up and sat down across from them. She was still afraid but at least she wasn't alone. Maybe the bear would eat the old man first, after all, he was much bigger. Then she could get away!

Just as she was thinking this, a mountain lion walked up and sat next to the bear. Then came a raccoon, followed by a coyote, and each of them took a place, forming a circle around her and the old man. The somewhat comforting thought she had had about getting away was gone. The animals were obviously having a party, and she and the old man were going to be their dinner! She was going to be eaten alive!

"This is Lost Girl," the Indian said, introducing her. "Lost Girl, these are my friends, Bear, Lion, Raccoon and Coyote." They each nodded their heads as their names were called.

She heard a flutter of wings and a loud caw. Raven landed on a branch that hung low over the old man's head.

The old man looked up with a grin. "Brother Raven! So glad that you could come!" He gave Courtney another little hug and winked. "Raven is one of the finest story tellers of all."

Terrific. She had run into the arms of a deranged old man who thought wild animals were his friends and ravens could talk. It had to be a nightmare. Any minute she would wake up in her own bed with Rags curled up beside her. *Oh please,* she thought, *let me wake up before they attack!*

But the animals didn't move. They just sat there with what appeared to be smiles on their faces. Why were they waiting? It was torture! She remembered that one night, after watching a particularly gruesome nature show on TV, her father had told her that if you were to be eaten by a wild animal, you went into shock and didn't feel a thing. Oh, why didn't they just get it over with?

"Today it is my turn to spin a tale," said the old man, looking around at the animals and then down at Courtney. "So, in honor of you, little lost one, I will tell the story of Rabbit Girl and The Three-Legged Fox."

The voice inside her screamed, *Wake up! Wake up!*

"Rabbit Girl was the youngest daughter of a great chief. She was very pretty, and she had everything a girl could ever want. But, still, she was always afraid something terrible was going to happen."

Courtney was sure she saw a beautiful, young Indian girl run past them like a frightened

deer. She could hear her heavy breathing and the twigs snapping beneath her feet. It was a dream. This whole thing was definitely a dream.

"One day, Rabbit Girl went off to gather berries," the old man went on, "and of course she got lost, just like she thought she would!

The trees pointed and called out, *This way! This way!* But she did not hear them.

The wind whispered of secret paths.

The creek sang to her, *Over here! Over here!*

The waterfall roared, *Go back! Go back!*

Even the rocks tried to turn her around by jabbing her feet, tripping her to make her stumble to her senses.

The winged ones and her four-legged brothers and sisters all tried to show her the way, but she paid them no mind. She was too afraid.

She was afraid she would fall down a ravine and tear her beautiful new dress on the bramble bushes. And so she did.

She was afraid black bears would steal her berry basket. And they did.

She was afraid she'd fall prey to a pack of hungry wolves. And the wolves surrounded her

But most of all, she was afraid she would meet the dreaded Three-Legged Fox. And of course, he showed up.

Rabbit Girl didn't know that it was the fox who told the wolves to go away because the moment she saw him, she fainted.

When she came to, she found herself lying on a soft buffalo robe in the lodge of the fox. The fox himself was inches away, his cold nose right in her face. He was inspecting her! Quickly, she sat up. But the fox kept on sniffing her and she was too scared to run.

The village story teller had told her many tales of the cunning Three-Legged Fox. He had lost his leg in a trap and was out for revenge. Three-Legged Fox was magic and there was no telling what he would do to her! Horrible things!

The fox completed his inspection and gave her a pointed look. It was really a very friendly look, but Rabbit Girl didn't see it that way. Then the fox turned and trotted out of the lodge.

At once, Rabbit Girl began thinking of how to escape.

But, the Three-Legged Fox was back in a flash. He had a piece of her torn dress in his mouth and he put it down in front of her. Again, he looked at her pointedly, turned and trotted off.

Rabbit Girl looked down at the piece of cloth, and then at her torn and dirty dress. What? Did he expect her to mend it?

At that very moment, the piece of cloth began to glow mysteriously, and right before her very eyes, it changed into a new dress! It was made of supple deerskin as white as the snow and was decorated with shimmering beads. It was the most beautiful dress she had ever seen. It had to be a trick. And she drew back from it.

Next, the fox brought her two scraps of leather. The leather glowed just as the cloth had, and instantly turned into a beautiful pair of moccasins.

The fox stared at her intently, trying to communicate. He twitched his ears. First the right one, then the left.

Rabbit Girl felt a strange, warm, tingling sensation from the top of her head to the tip of her toes. Suddenly, she was wearing the new clothes! She hadn't put them on, they just appeared on her! She felt her hair. It was combed and braided, tied with beaded bands!

The fox looked at her, his eyes flashing with satisfaction, and off he went again.

Many gifts Three-Legged Fox gave her. Jewelry, a feathered fan, a beaded pouch. He brought her food to eat and provided for her every need. He even promised to guide her home in the morning. But she didn't understand him. Still, she was afraid. She was sure Fox had other plans for her. Terrible plans.

That night, Rabbit Girl waited for the fox to fall asleep. Quietly, she tiptoed past him, ducked out, and ran away.

She had no idea that he was right behind her. But she should have known that a magic fox never sleeps.

She ran and ran, until she could run no more. Then she lay down under a cottonwood tree and had a rest.

When she opened her eyes the next morning, the fox was there, waiting patiently, staring

at her. This time his look was not so friendly. Rabbit Girl had insulted his kindness and he was going to teach her a lesson.

Rabbit Girl jumped to her feet and backed up against the tree. She felt that strange tingling sensation again, but this time it was cold. Her body felt like it was shrinking. She was collapsing in on herself! Suddenly she was very small and everything around her was huge.

Three-Legged Fox had turned her into a rabbit!"

Courtney looked up at the old man with a worried expression. "Did he eat her?"

"No, he didn't eat her," the old one laughed. Then he paused dramatically, looking around at his animal brothers who anxiously waited with looks on their faces that said: *Come on, tell us what happened?!*

Finally, the old man laughed again and continued. "Quick as a bunny, which is what she was, Rabbit Girl hopped away, jumped in a burrow and hid! She had to hide there for a very long time."

Courtney was no longer worried about the animals attacking. She didn't care whether this was all a dream, or a nightmare, or real. The only thing that concerned her was the story and what would happen next.

"Three-Legged Fox busied himself, digging a hole near the burrow. Once it was dug to his satisfaction, he rested, keeping watch. He knew that Rabbit Girl would come out in time. And he was right.

It wasn't very comfortable for her inside. It was dark and damp, cold and cramped, and since she hadn't touched any of the food Fox had brought her, she was absolutely starving as well! Before too long Rabbit Girl got tired of being afraid. She decided that even death would be better than this. And she boldly hopped out of the burrow.

"So you have finally come out to face me," said the Three-Legged Fox with a grin.

This time Rabbit Girl understood him. She looked him straight in the eye. "It is a good day to..." her voice trailed off with a tremble, her little pink nose twitched. But before she could say "die", that strange sensation came over her and she felt herself growing.

The fox had changed her back into a girl again. She hugged herself thankfully.

Three-Legged Fox had only meant to give her a teaching. He came to her, and she knelt down and hugged him, stroking his velvet-soft fur.

Fox licked her face affectionately. Then he looked deeply into her eyes and said, "You have learned well, Rabbit Girl. Now breathe all your fears into the hole I have dug and we will bury them in the earth as a giveaway."

And so they did."

The animals in the circle all smiled and nodded their approval. It was a good story.

"Did she ever find her way home?" Courtney wanted to know. It was important.

"Of course she did," replied the old man, "without fear, she could be guided."

Courtney became aware of a scratching sound. Bear was digging a hole. She studied him for a moment, then looked up at the old man. "Why is he doing that?" she asked, and then glanced back at Bear. "It's for my fears, isn't it?"

"Ha ha! See that? You are hearing better already!" the old man chuckled.

Courtney got up slowly from her place beside him and walked toward the hole. Bear stood beside it, waiting. She hesitated. She felt fear's cold fingers tightening around her throat.

Bear seemed to understand. He moved back and sat down, trying to make himself look as small and unintimidating as possible. He cocked his big head like a puppy.

Courtney couldn't help but giggle. Bear looked like a huge stuffed toy. She moved in timidly and looked into the hole.

"Think it's big enough to hold them all?" the old man called to her.

Courtney looked at the old man tentatively, then looked around at the animals. They were smiling at her encouragingly. Courtney looked back into the hole. She knew what she had to do.

She took a deep breath, and thought about all her fears, from the littlest to the biggest. Gym class, piano recitals, nightmares, the dentist. What if she got an F in math? What if the other kids laughed at her 'cause she did something dumb? What if her parents got a divorce?!

The terrible "what ifs" tore through her mind like angry demons. But she let them go and she blew them all into the hole.

She thought about all the horrible things she had ever seen on TV, and she blew.

She thought about all the terrible things her parents talked about... war, disease, the economy! Crime, pollution, and the ozone layer. Mass murderers and airplane crashes! She thought about earthquakes and thunderstorms and strangers.

She blew, and she blew, until every scary thing she ever thought was swept away and her mind was as clean as her mother's kitchen after maid's day. Then she covered the hole with dirt.

Her body felt so light she thought for a minute she just might float away. And the thought didn't scare her in the least! Amazing! With a glowing smile, she turned to her new friends.

Bear was waving his arms as if applauding. Mountain lion purred. Coyote let out a happy little howl. Raccoon ran round and round in giddy little circles. And Raven cawed gleefully. "You have done well," the old Indian said with a Cheshire cat grin.

Just then the wind kicked up in a loud gust.

"The wind is talking to you," the old man said.

Courtney listened. The wind died down to a gentle whisper and she could hear a voice calling in the distance.

"Courtney! Court!"

59

Then she heard another.

"Court-ney!"

It was her mom and dad! Then she heard Rags barking.

"Rags!" she cried out in excitement, and she ran out of the clearing.

Almost at once however, she remembered her manners and hurried back. "Thank you very much," she said from the bottom of her heart. "I really hope I see you again." She looked around at the animals. "All of you," she smiled. And she meant it.

The animals and the old man all waved good-bye. Courtney felt tears welling up in her eyes. Maybe she would never see them again, but she would never forget. She waved back, then turned and hurried off.

She followed the wind that called, *This way! This way!*

The trees bent down their boughs and pointed.

The creek sang.

And Hawk flew overhead, just to be sure.

Soon she was in her parents' arms and they were hugging her and Rags was jumping up and down, licking her face.

Her mother was crying. "Courtney, oh sweetheart, thank God you're all right!"

"Poor baby, you must have been scared to death!" Her dad cooed sympathetically.

She couldn't wait to tell them about the old Indian man and the animals. "I was scared but then I..."

But her parents didn't hear her, or didn't want to. Her mother grabbed her by the arm, and they headed for the car. "I'm telling you, you had us so worried, Courtney!" she said, not even looking back at her. "We thought... Oh never mind what we thought, it's too awful!"

"But, Mom..."

"We have every ranger in the county out looking for you," her father interjected, glancing over his shoulder at her as if it was all her fault.

"I told you this was a mistake, Bruce," her mom went on. "Didn't I tell you something terrible was going to happen? Didn't I?! You know, this kind of early childhood experience could scar her for life!"

"Okay, okay. I'll set up an appointment with the therapist." Her father opened the car door. "Hop in, Court."

"But, Daddy," she pleaded, "there's something I want to tell you and Mom."

Her mom was already in the car, getting out the laptop.

"Sure, Court, you can tell us later," he said, hustling her into her seat, "right now I'm going to get us back to the good old city!" And he slammed the door. "Buckle up!"

Buckle up all right! They weren't very far down the road and already her dad was singing loudly to the radio and her mom was tap, tap, tapping away. It was back to real life with the worried worker and the lounge lizard. Maybe it had all been a dream. Well, at least she had

Rags. She stared out of the window and sighed.

Then she saw something that made her heart light.

Standing by the road sign that said WATCH FOR ANIMALS NEXT 40 MILES, was the old man and in his arms he held a three-legged fox!

Courtney broke into a smile. "Mom, Dad," her voice sounded different somehow. "Wanna hear a story? It's a good one!"

Bruce looked in the rear view mirror. His voice caught in his throat. He blinked in disbelief.

Beverly gasped...

In the back seat of their car sat a stranger with bold flashing eyes.

In the back seat of their car sat Rabbit Girl.

PART
III

THE GIVEAWAY

The girl with golden hair laughed. She had a new twinkle in her eye. "Do you know what my name is, Grandfather?" she asked teasingly.

"Yes," the old one nodded. "You are Girl-With-Golden-Hair."

"No," the girl giggled. "My name is Courtney!"

"No!" Grandfather feigned a look of shock. "What a coincidence!"

"My parents are Bruce and Beverly," Courtney went on, "and they are just like you said, and I have a dog named Rags and everything!" Her words tumbled one over another in excitement. "I was in the story, I really was, and so were you! You are the old man in the stories, aren't you, Grandfather?"

Grandfather chuckled but he didn't exactly answer her. "What we see on the outside is just a mirror of what we think on the inside," was all he said.

None of the children were sure they really understood what he meant, but it didn't matter. They all knew he was the old man he told of.

Grandfather looked at the brown-skinned boy who sat to his right, then gestured around the circle with the hawk feather. "On the Medicine Wheel are four directions, each holding different lessons. As we move around the wheel of life, we are changed. That is the way of Nature. The seasons come, the seasons go. The seed becomes a tree."

Grandfather handed the hawk feather to the boy. "The old," he said with a nod, "must always giveaway to the new."

"It is in such changing times, this story begins," Grandfather continued, "a time we called the Dog Days."

"Why the Dog Days, Grandfather?" the brown-skinned boy asked.

"Because in those days, so long ago, the people depended on Dog for many things. And Dog was loyal and unselfish. This was his medicine.

Dog guarded their camps, entertained their children and kept them warm. But, most important of all, dog was their beast of burden. He helped them carry their belongings from place to place as they moved in search of better game.

There was discord brewing over just this issue in the camp of Sees Far. Moving.

The camp was a small one, not more than a dozen teepees. They were set up in a circle just within sight of the Sacred Mountain that loomed up so unexpectedly from the expanse of rolling land that surrounded them. It was usually a happy camp, for the most part, but these days a cold wind was blowing.

Everyday, Sees Far would sit in front of his teepee

and wait. He watched the children at play and the women at work. There were few cook fires for there was little to cook. Game was hunted out and his people were thin and hungry. It was time to move. But still, Sees Far waited.

Everyday his wife, Wind Song, would nag him. All the women in the camp wanted to move. They were tired of having so little to feed their families. All the men in the camp wanted to move. They were tired of coming home from the hunt empty-handed, tired of hearing their wives complain and their children cry with hunger. The top of Sacred Mountain was white with snow. Soon all the land would be too. It was time.

But Sees Far had been their chief for as long as anyone could remember, and he insisted that they stay. Spirit voices had told him a great gift would be given them, and they had to wait.

Everyone thought he was crazy. They talked about him in their teepees at night. Could be the old chief was dying. Old ones often lost their minds and behaved in strange ways right before death. The voices he heard were probably his ancestors calling him. The gift was surely his own passing. Maybe they should leave him behind and move on before they all died with him. In the whole camp only one person believed in Sees Far and his spirit voices. Lame Dog.

The people considered Lame Dog to be less than the four-leggeds whose name he bore. He was an orphan, skinny and crippled. In their minds, he was good for nothing except hauling wood and water.

Sees Far, however, loved the boy, and treated him as his son. He and the men had found him as a baby, near dead, out on the Great Plains, one leg pitifully twisted. No one could guess what had happened to his parents or his tribe, for they had left not a trace, not a track, not a single clue. The men had wanted to leave him there. They were sure that the dying child's own people had abandoned him for good reason. Sees Far did not agree. "This child holds good medicine," he declared. So he brought the tiny orphan home, and he and Wind Song nursed him.

For many moons he lay sick and delirious with fever. Then just when Sees Far and Wind Song were beginning to give up all hope, he recovered. But his twisted leg did not heal, and he was to be cursed forever to walk with a limp.

Thirteen summers had now passed. Lame Dog was almost a man. Although he was slight in stature, he was strong and he was very handsome. Nonetheless, because of his disability, no one paid him any attention except to order him to fetch them water or bring them wood. No one except the old chief and his wife, and a young girl named Little Feather.

The girl often found herself watching Lame Dog as he moved around the camp. She felt more than just pity for him and every time their eyes met, she would give him a smile.

Lame Dog thought she was beautiful, and she was indeed, everyone thought so. Her hair was as black as a raven's wing, her round, dancing eyes were light, like polished agate flecked with gold, and full of kindness. And her smile! Her smile was magic, so radiant it could surely turn an angry bear into a bowl of mush. Oh, how Lame Dog wanted her, but he knew that only in his dreams would she be his.

Whenever he was called to bring water or wood to her teepee, his heart would flutter like a hundred skylarks and he would try to look taller and walk faster, hoping to receive the gift of her smile. But most of the time he watched her from afar, and the smiles they exchanged were few, for Little Feather's mother kept her away from him. A dog was not good enough for her daughter. Her daughter would someday become wife to Tails-In-The-Air.

Tails-In-The-Air was only a few summers older than Lame Dog and already he had become leader of the hunt because of his ability with a bow. Already he was one of the most important men in the tribe.

Lame Dog didn't stand a chance.

At last, one bitterly cold day, the men came back from another hunt. Again they returned with nothing and they were angry.

They didn't stop at their teepees to greet their wives and children. Moving in a tight group, like the thunderheads of a coming monsoon, they marched straight over to the teepee of Sees Far.

Lame Dog was sitting next to the old chief and he cast his eyes down and shrank back, hoping not to be noticed, especially by Tails-In-The-Air who took every opportunity to tease and belittle him.

But Tails-In-The-Air was too angry and too full of himself to pay any mind to Lame Dog. He confronted the chief. "Our game bags are empty," he cried. "Winter is coming, the people are starving! When will you put an end to this foolishness? Do you want us all to die for your spirit voices?!"

The men all chuckled at the mention of the voices.

Sees Far sat still as stone and stared at them. He was unmoved. Finally he spoke. His words were clear. "The gift will come. We must wait."

"Your voices are wrong!" Tails-In-The-Air challenged angrily. "Your voices are destroying our people! We must move!"

Of course Tails-In-The-Air had another motive for wanting the move. He cared about his people, yes, but he also thought he was most likely to become chief when Sees Far died and he was eager for that day to come. The chief was old and weak and crazy! He would not do well on a move, and Tails-In-The-Air knew that. So he argued and he argued.

But the old chief could not be swayed. "The voices have told me we must wait, and wait we will," he said with command. "You will go on another hunt. If again you come back with nothing, you are free to go without me." The chief made a gesture of finality and the argument was over. It was agreed that the men would get some rest and leave the following day.

Tails-In-The-Air and the men turned and walked off sullenly. Lame Dog breathed a sigh of relief.

"Tails-In-The-Air!" the old chief suddenly called.

The young brave turned, hoping that the chief had reconsidered.

But what Sees Far said only made the men laugh.

"This time you will take Lame Dog with you."

"Lame Dog?! You are crazy!" Tails-In-The-Air jeered, doubling over with laughter. "What good would he be on a hunt? He is a dog! And a lame one at that! He can't even walk! It would be better to take a woman!" Then, much to the delight of the other men, Tails-In-The-Air did an imitation of Lame Dog, walking with an exaggerated limp, pulling a bow string and stumbling.

The men all laughed uproariously, pointing at Lame Dog in ridicule.

Lame Dog stared at the ground and wished that it would swallow him up. How could Sees Far have suggested such a thing?

Just at that moment, Wind Song came charging out of the teepee, wielding a stick and yelling, "Go! Go, you fleas!" She was not about to stand for that kind of cruel mockery! Wind Song was a feisty old one, and if she came after you, you'd better get out of the way fast! The men did.

She watched after them for a few seconds, waving the stick threateningly, to be sure they didn't come back. Finally she turned and glared angrily at her husband, then stormed back inside the teepee, closing the hide flap with a loud slap as if she was slamming a door. She was not at all happy with the whole situation, and she blamed it all on him. Stubborn old man! He and his voices! Now his lunacy had brought humiliation to Lame Dog and this was too much. She vowed not to speak to him for an entire moon!

Lame Dog tossed and turned all night, sleeping little. The scoffing laughter of the men rang through his head, tormenting him. By dawn's break he had made a decision.

He would go on a hunt alone. He would bring back lots of game and be a hero! Then no one would ever laugh at him again! He thought of the smile he would get from Little Feather, then he took Sees Far's bow and quiver and silently crept out of the teepee.

He was long gone before anyone knew it."

"That's just what I would have done," the brown-skinned boy interjected, as Grandfather paused.

"I know," the old man said softly.

The boy looked down. "I get teased and laughed at too, because of my color."

Grandfather lifted the boy's head and looked deeply into his dark eyes. "Your color is something to be proud of," he said.

"It doesn't seem that way," the boy retorted, "but someday I'm going to prove myself, just like Lame Dog!"

"Of that I am sure," the old one smiled.

"Lame Dog traveled across the bleak land for a great distance. There was no game to be found. The sun had passed its apex. The air was devoid of the sound of birds and the cold wind stung at his face. The signs of impending winter were everywhere, and with each step he took his hopes were reduced.

But at last, at the edge of a wooded place near the river he spotted two turkeys!

Slowly, he pulled an arrow from the quiver and readied the bow. Then, just as Sees Far had taught him, he whispered a special prayer and politely asked the two turkeys to giveaway their lives to him.

He smiled to himself. Turkeys were always willing to giveaway.

Not these two.

Lame Dog lowered the bow with a sigh as the two big birds flapped away awkwardly into the woods, gobbling in protest.

Lame Dog decided to head into the woods too. Maybe there were more turkeys in there. Maybe a whole tribe!

No. The woods seemed empty of all life, silent save for the wind that blew through the bare trees, whistling a forlorn song.

Yet the determined boy went on, and after a time, he finally came across a rabbit.

Again he carefully prepared the bow and drew back the string. Again he softly said his prayer. "Oh please giveaway to me, Sister Rabbit," he added, "my people need food."

But Rabbit did not want to giveaway either. "I really would like to oblige you, brown-skinned boy," she said wiggling her nose, "but I have children at home who need me."

Wind Song had taught him how to talk to animals and how to understand them by listening with his heart. He couldn't shoot the rabbit even though she sat there motionless, an easy target. "Go on, little sister," he said, shooing her off with the bow.

Rabbit hopped away thankfully, and Lame Dog again went on. He was most discouraged.

Suddenly, he heard a loud cawing. He looked up to see Raven fluttering down to land in a tree just in front of him.

"You are a good boy!" she cawed. "But that little rabbit was nothing but a snack anyway! Keep on going and your charity will be rewarded. Keep on going and you will find yourself a real meal!" Then she laughed raucously and flew away.

Lame Dog wondered why she had laughed so uproariously but he took her advice anyway and he kept on going.

Raven had not lied. He did not have to go far before he came almost face to face with a huge buffalo!

Lame Dog smiled broadly. The buffalo was old and weak. He stood there swaying back and forth as if he were going to drop at any minute.

Once more, Lame Dog readied his bow. "Brother Buffalo," he said, "you are very old and I have come to help you to the other side so you may join your ancestors." And then he started to say his prayer. But before he could finish it, old Brother Buffalo let out a mighty bellow and charged at him!

Limping and stumbling, Lame Dog ran, and, not until he reached the edge of the Great Plains did he stop.

Only wanting to scare the boy who had prayed to him so nicely, the old buffalo had given up long ago. Still Lame Dog looked back just to be sure, then finally sat down to rest. The sun was sinking and so were his spirits. No one would giveaway to him, not even a dying buffalo.

The first evening star was twinkling high above the horizon. Soon the sky people would unfold the dark canopy of night. He would have to go back to camp empty-handed. And he would have to take punishment for stealing Sees Far's bow and quiver.

With a heavy heart, Lame Dog looked out over the Great Plains, a vast stretch of nothing. Why had he so foolishly thought he could bring home game when all the men had failed?

He was getting up to leave when he noticed a teepee way off in the distance, smoke curling up from its smoke hole. For a second, his heart stopped. He blinked his eyes. He had been staring out at the plains for quite some time. The teepee had not been there before, he was sure of it. How could it appear like that, so suddenly?

He started walking towards it, though he didn't know why, because it was in the opposite direction from camp. He had no choice, the teepee drew him like a magnet.

Stranger than that, the closer he came to it, the closer it came to him! It was as if the teepee was moving toward him; and before long he was standing right in front of it!

Lame Dog stared in awe. The teepee was made from soft hides stained with many colors and painted with symbols... strange symbols of stick men on top of dog-like animals. *What do they mean?* he wanted to know, for he had never seen anything like them. He also wanted to know why the teepee had appeared to move, and why it wasn't there and then was. He decided to find out.

He called out a greeting to whoever was inside, but no one answered. He moved in closer and called out once more. Again, not a sound came from the teepee. Sees Far had told him about visions. Could this be one? Cautiously, he went to the door flap, bent down and looked in.

There was no one inside! Buffalo robes were spread all around. A fire was going and over it hung a big cook pot. A savory aroma took over his senses, and he remembered how long it had been since he had eaten. *I'll only eat a little bit,* he thought. Whatever was cooking was so enticing, he couldn't help himself. He started in.

Just then, a deep voice spoke, startling him so that he tripped over himself and fell flat on his face.

"Come in and rest, grandson," said the voice.

Lame Dog looked up. Sitting by the cook pot, where no one had been a moment before, was an ancient-looking man with long white hair and turquoise eyes, and he was ladling out a bowl of the delicious-smelling stew.

81

He smiled at Lame Dog kindly. "I've prepared some food for you," he said.

The old one spoke the language of the animals, talking without talking, and Lame Dog understood.

With a nod, he handed the dumbstruck boy the bowl of stew. The boy devoured it, gulping it down voraciously, smiling and nodding at the old man all at the same time. Gone were the questions he wanted to ask. All he could think of was filling his belly. It was the tastiest food he had ever eaten, full of succulent pieces of meat, wild greens and seasonings.

The old man dipped the ladle in the pot and filled the bowl again. "Eat as much as you like," he said. "You have a great task ahead of you."

Lame Dog ate four bowls of the stew, one right after another, and then he felt sleepy. So sleepy he could hardly keep his eyes open. He vaguely recalled wanting to ask questions but somehow he couldn't remember what they were.

The old one smiled and lit his pipe. "Tomorrow you will travel a day's journey to the east," he whispered at last. "There you will find the gift."

And Lame Dog fell into a deep slumber.

When he opened his eyes, the sun had already risen and he found himself curled up on the hard ground of the naked plain. How did he get there? He remembered nothing! He stared up at the still blue sky.

Then slowly, it all began to come back to him, the mocking laughter of the men, stealing

Sees Far's quiver and bow and leaving camp. He remembered the turkeys and the rabbit, the raven and the buffalo. Suddenly he realized that his hand was clutching something round and hard. He uncurled his fingers... it was a stone, and on it a symbol was painted, a stick-like man on top of a... dog?

Lame Dog sat up as if a bolt of lightning had hit him. He looked around.

There was no sign of the old man, not even a mark where the teepee had been. Then he heard a voice in his head, so clearly that there was no mistaking it.

Journey to the east. There you will find the gift.

Lame Dog put the stone in his medicine pouch and headed toward the rising sun.

He limped along for mile after mile of desolate, windswept prairie. The sun climbed higher and higher in the sky. Why was he doing this? he asked himself. He was getting further and further away from camp. Maybe he would never find his way back! Maybe he would die out here alone on the Great Plains, just as he had almost died as an infant. Was that his unavoidable fate?

He thought about Sees Far sitting by the fire, telling stories of great warriors and talking animals. He thought about Wind Song bent over the cook pot, trying to make something out of nothing, singing even when there was nothing to sing about. He thought about Little Feather's smile. But the thoughts rolled through his mind and blew away like tumbleweeds, and the voice within drove him on... *You will find the gift. You will find the gift.*"

The brown-skinned boy felt strangely dizzy. Just as the other children had experienced before him, Grandfather's voice was beginning to fade. He held the hawk feather tightly. It was as if the old man was awakening some ancient memory of another time deep within him. He no longer needed to hear the words, it was like he was remembering.

Lame Dog hardly noticed that he was steadily climbing. His throat was dry and he had no water. He was hungry and he had no food. *You will find the gift,* the voice kept repeating. Nothing else mattered.

At last he came to a spring bubbling up with clear, icy cold water. He lay down, dunked his head in it and drank. Once he had his fill, he got to his feet and sat back on his haunches.

Looming up before him, glowing golden in the afternoon sun, was Sacred Mountain!

Lame Dog looked around in excitement.

He had reached the top of a steep hill. Below him was a small valley surrounded by the mountain's rocky foothills. The sun was directly behind him, casting long shadows, and he suddenly realized he had been traveling all day. Something about that realization struck him but he couldn't quite grasp what it was. More troublesome thoughts took over, like where he would he sleep that night and what would he do to feed himself? Then the voice screamed, *the gift, the gift!* And he started down the hill.

At first he only heard them, and the sound made him stop dead in his tracks.

They came into the valley on thundering hooves, a whole herd of them, and their power made the ground quake beneath his feet. They were as swift coming as a winter storm, and moved with the grace of deer and the strength of buffalo. They looked like stags who had lost their horns. But they were not stags. They had long necks and tails, and flowing manes that streamed like prayer cloths in the wind. And they were many colored! There were blacks and whites and browns, greys and reds, even one was gold. Lame Dog could hardly believe his eyes. They were like no creatures he had ever seen!

Soon the strange animals settled and began grazing on the few patches of green that still dotted the valley floor. Lame Dog crept in closer, being most careful not to alarm them. Just one of these creatures would feed the whole camp! And there were so many of them, surely one would giveaway to him. He drew out an arrow.

The gold one who appeared to be their leader, stopped grazing and looked over in Lame Dog's direction.

Lame Dog held his breath.

The great beast's muscles were taut, quivering under his skin. His coat glistened like honey in the last rays of the fading sun. He was magnificent!

Lame Dog's first thought came from his

heart... he couldn't kill such a beautiful animal! The second, more practical thought, came from his mind... and if he did, how would he get it back to camp? These animals were as big as elks! Lame Dog sank down in dismay.

The honey-colored leader seemed to sense that the danger had passed. He shook his head, tossing his great white mane, stretched his long neck and began nibbling at the grass again.

Lame Dog stared at him in wonder. Suddenly, the dogs flashed into his mind... pulling travois! That was it! One of these animals could easily pull as much weight as ten dogs! The idea excited him so much that he jumped to his feet.

The leader lifted his head and looked around, wild-eyed, nostrils flaring. He made a strange sound and began prancing around urgently, alerting the others.

Within seconds the herd was thundering out of the valley.

Lame Dog hobbled after them, following in the wake of dust that trailed behind them. Now all he had to do was catch one! He gave no thought as to how he would do it. He had found the gift!

"Horses," the brown-skinned boy whispered, not knowing it.

"Yes," Grandfather nodded. And then he continued. "By dusk, Lame Dog had lost sight of the horses, but his heart was singing. Though he knew not what to call them, he knew beyond a

87

shadow of a doubt, that he would find them again.

That night an old rabbit gaveaway to him. He found shelter in a cave, built a cook fire and filled his belly. Then he fell asleep thinking of the honey-colored stallion, and his dreams were sweet.

The next morning he started out early. There had been a great wind that night which awakened him several times. He knew that tracks would now be hard to find, so he decided to stick to the high ground where he could see for greater distances.

He spotted them from the rim of a box canyon, the honey-colored stallion and the rest of the herd, milling around lazily, drinking from a small stream that cut through it.

At the far end of the canyon there was a narrow opening. Other than that there was no way out. Silently, Lame Dog made his way toward it, limping cautiously so as not to disturb a single bush or stone.

Just above the opening, a huge dead tree clung perilously to the rocky canyon wall. Lame Dog's heart leapt. If he could loosen it enough to make it fall, it might create a barricade! He slid down to it, his heart pounding with excitement, and set to work at once. He tried to work as quietly as he could.

At first the horses didn't seem to notice, then the stallion started trotting around nervously, arousing the others. Lame Dog had to do something fast. He pushed at the tree with all his might, but it still wouldn't budge.

Then he took a chance. At the top of his voice, he screamed. Great spirit was with him. Instead of running for the opening, the frightened horses bolted off toward the other end of the canyon.

Lame Dog worked furiously now, digging and pushing, throwing rock after rock aside with no care as to how much noise he made. The tree creaked, its roots were snapping, soon it would fall. Soon.

But then the horses came, running fast from the far end of the canyon toward the opening, the stallion behind them, nipping at their rumps, driving them forward.

In a frenzy, Lame Dog pushed. He pushed with his feet, he pushed with his hands, he pushed with every bit of strength he had.

One after another, the horses escaped.

And Lame Dog kept pushing. Suddenly he felt an incredible force enter his body. He braced his feet against the tree and pushed once more. With a final creaking groan, the tree gave way!

It fell with a crash and a rumble, taking rocks and dirt with it.

When the dust settled, there was but one horse left trapped in the canyon. The honey-colored stallion!

Lame Dog's heart was beating like a war dance drum. He fell to his knees and kissed the Earth, his mother, then he opened his arms to Father Sky. "Thank you," he shouted from the

89

core of his being. "Thank you!"

The great horse reared up on his hind legs and pawed the air, letting out an agonized, bleating scream, then he wheeled about and began running around the canyon, frantically looking for another way out. Finding none, he returned to the blocked opening and stomped at the ground. He looked up at Lame Dog, his eyes blazing with hatred, and then he turned with a snort and ran off.

Lame dog did nothing but watch for a while. He had the golden animal trapped, now what?

The stallion moved around the canyon restlessly. Moving, moving, never stopping. *If only he would stand still, maybe I could communicate with him*, Lame Dog thought. Then the voice spoke to him: *Keep him moving!* it said. "Keep him moving!"

With a resounding war cry, Lame Dog leapt from his perch to the canyon floor.

The startled horse bolted and ran. Lame Dog could not possibly keep up with him so he dogged him instead, hobbling and hopping around the edge of the canyon, jumping down in front of him from the rocks, never allowing the horse a moment's rest.

All afternoon and all through the night, the chase went on. Neither horse nor boy rested or took nourishment. Every muscle in the boy's body ached but he ignored the pain and kept on going.

Finally, as the first rays of morning sun crept into the canyon, Lame Dog sank to his knees in exhaustion.

Twenty yards away, the stallion stood, staring at him, soaked with sweat, vapor blowing from his nostrils. He looked exhausted too. But, suddenly, with no warning, he charged.

Lame Dog scrambled to his feet in terror. The stallion was coming at him like an angry bull, like the buffalo had, but faster. There was fire in his eyes. Lame Dog stumbled towards the rocks at the edge of the canyon. But then, his bad leg gave under him and he fell.

At once, the stallion was on him, rearing up and crying savagely. Lame Dog rolled out of the way just before his hooves struck, and crawled to the safety of the rocks.

He pulled himself up to a small flat ledge and there he fell back, gasping for breath. He stared up at the morning sky. *Oh, Grandfather, please, help me,* he silently cried, and then he closed his eyes.

It felt as though he had slept for hours, but in fact, it was only a moment or two. His body no longer ached and he felt no fatigue. He sat up and scanned the canyon. The horse was gone! But that couldn't be!

And then he looked down.

The stallion stood next to the rocks, almost directly below him. *How perfect!* Lame Dog quietly got to his feet and prepared to leap down in front of him.

Was it by chance? Or was it Great Spirit's intervention? In any case, when Lame Dog jumped, the horse moved just enough, and Lame Dog landed on his back!

The surprised stallion let out a terrified cry and immediately bolted. Lame Dog threw his

arms around his neck and held on for dear life. Round and round the canyon the horse took him, bucking and rearing like a rodeo bronco. Again and again he bucked and reared and reared and bucked. And at last, he threw him.

Lame Dog landed on the hard ground with a thud. He sat up in a daze, his head spinning.

The stallion stood not far away looking at him challengingly, but he did not move.

The boy tried to get to his feet but the wind was gone from him and he could not. It was then that he noticed his medicine pouch lying on the ground next to him. The leather tie that had held it was broken. It must have fallen from him sometime during the chase. He picked it up, then felt the round, hard object inside and he remembered. He dumped it out into his hand. Now the symbol spoke to him. Now the light dawned! His strength was renewed. With excitement he rose to his feet and returned the stallion's challenge.

Slowly he moved. Again, the stallion bolted. And so the chase began again and went on until afternoon.

Then at last, the great stallion gave up. His endurance was spent, his power drained from him. He swayed unsteadily like a newborn colt then dropped to his knees and rolled onto his side.

Lame Dog dropped too, and he watched, waiting for the horse to get up. But the great animal did not stir. Slowly, Lame Dog crawled over to him.

The stallion was heaving and covered in froth. He lifted his head with effort and looked at the boy. His eyes were no longer wild. Then he let his head fall.

He was defeated.

Lame Dog touched him gently and began to stroke him, wiping away the foam. He stroked his head and his neck, he stroked his back, he massaged his withers. And he sang. *Cheda-e, Na-kahu-kahu, Be-be, Cheda-e, Nakahu-kahu, Be-be.* It was the song Wind Song so often sang to him and it always soothed him. *Go to sleep, Baby dear, slumber, Baby.*

Long into the night, with love, he sang... and he stroked, his hands never still, his song never ending.

Cheda-e, Nakahu-kahu, Be-be."

"In the days that followed, Lame Dog became one with the horse and the horse became one with him. Soon he was riding on his back as if he had been born there. What matter did one twisted leg make when he had four beneath him! Now, back at the camp of Sees Far... "

"Grandfather," the brown-skinned boy interrupted, shaking his head for the memory was fading. "How did they get out of the canyon? They did get out, didn't they?"

"Of course they did," Grandfather replied with a chuckle. "They jumped over the barrier."

"But, Grandfather, if the stallion could jump over it, why didn't he do that before?"

"It sometimes takes horses a while to figure things out," the old man said, and then he paused, nodding his head the way he always did, as if he knew some great secret no one else knew. "I think Great Spirit clouded his mind a little."

Satisfied with the explanation, the brown-skinned boy smiled and nodded in agreement.

Then Grandfather went on. "So, back at the camp, nearly a moon had passed and all hope for the return of Lame Dog had been abandoned. Tails-In-The-Air was happy, the people were getting ready to move. Their teepees had been folded, their belongings were packed. Even Wind Song had decided to leave. She was fed up with her husband's stubbornness and broken-hearted over the loss of Lame Dog.

Only the teepee of Sees Far remained standing, and the old chief sat in front of it. Still, Sees Far waited.

The people were hitching the dogs to the travois when they heard the thundering sound and looked up.

Across the rolling plain, the horses came like a stampeding herd of buffalo.

The people dropped what they were doing. They stared in awe for a moment, then scattered in fear.

Sees Far did not move. He just watched.

It was Tails-In-The-Air who first saw Lame Dog. He froze in his tracks. His mouth fell open in shock.

Lame Dog was riding on the back of one of the animals! He was charging through the herd as if the wind were carrying him, whooping and waving his arms.

The herd slowed down and began milling around the outskirts of what had once been the camp. But the golden one carrying Lame Dog kept coming and he didn't stop until he reached Tails-In-The-Air.

Tails-In-The-Air looked up at Lame Dog who towered above him, sitting tall and proud on the back of the strange animal. It was not a cowering dog who sat there, it was a man. Lame Dog spoke not a word. He didn't have to. The look he gave Tails-In-The-Air said all there was to say.

Tails-In-The-Air was humbled.

Little Feather came forward, her eyes sparkling. She looked up at Lame Dog and gave him the most radiant smile she had ever given.

And her mother did not stop her.

Lame Dog returned her smile and dismounted. They gazed into each others eyes with promise, lost, for what seemed an eternity.

Then Lame Dog turned and walked to Sees Far's teepee where the old chief sat waiting. And the honey-colored stallion followed.

The old man rose to his feet to meet them, tears in his eyes.

"This is for you, my father," Lame Dog said, stroking the stallion's neck. "A big dog."

Sees Far embraced him. And Wind Song ran to him and embraced him too. Then she embraced her husband. She would never doubt him again.

Just as the old chief had foretold, the great gift was given.

It was a gift that would change their lives forever. A gift for all the people, as all great gifts should be."

The children, Andy, Courtney and the brown-skinned boy, John, sat silently a long time.

Then, as they watched in wonder, Hawk made a low circle above them and glided down to land on Grandfather's shoulder.

"Everything is a circle," the old man finally said, "like the medicine wheel, a teaching. But to gain the teaching you must be able to see, like Hawk here, from all perspectives."

Grandfather picked up a large stone and set it in the very center of the wheel.

"You each see this stone from a different angle," he said. "You each have heard the stories in your own way, yet we all sit in the same circle."

He looked around at each of the children, nodding in that knowing way. "Fear will blind you and deafen your ears. You must become warriors against it. Then you will see the truth. Then you will be ready to give a great gift to the people, for then you will know that, under the color of our skin, our fur or our feathers, we are all one."

The children nodded, for this day, they had gained understanding.

Grandfather smiled.

And just then, something fantastic happened. Something so wonderful it made them gasp...

Out of thin air, the honey-colored stallion slowly appeared behind Grandfather. It was as if the horse had stepped right out of the story, and he was the most beautiful and perfect horse any of them had ever seen. His shining coat was as golden as the sun and his snow-white mane was tied with ribbons and eagle feathers.

The stallion whinnied softly, lowered his great head and nudged Grandfather gently on the cheek.

The old man reached up and stroked his neck. "Yes, Big Dog," he said, "it is time." And he got to his feet.

The stunned children found their voices and began to protest. "Please, Grandfather, don't go," they pleaded. "Stay just a while longer, please."

Grandfather looked down at them, smiling. "One part of a whole thing can never be without the others. I am in your heart and you are in mine... always." With that he mounted the stallion and rode away, and Hawk followed, flying over his head.

The children watched until they could see them no more and then turned to leave.

It was Hawk's distant cry that made them turn back and look up.

There, in the painted clouds of the sunset, they saw Grandfather and the honey-colored stallion riding across the sky. They heard the stallion whinny, and Grandfather waved. Then the clouds closed around them and they disappeared.

The children stared at the sunset until it had faded, hoping to catch another glimpse of them. Then finally, just as the crickets and frogs were beginning their night songs and the sky people were lighting the stars, they started down the hill. They promised each other that they would never tell what had happened that day for surely no one would ever believe them. And then they walked in silence for there was nothing more to say.

Somehow they knew they would never see him again. But each of them was forever changed, and none of them would ever forget Grandfather's good medicine.

For their devoted consultation, brilliant insight, editorial
feedback and loving support, heartfelt thanks to:
My sisters, Dev Ross and Nadia,
Mama and Laughing Old Pop,
Kate Thorne and Lynn Edwards.

Also To:
Michael Horse, Raymond Kane, Redwing, Elray Deroin,
Bearheart, T.C. Ahkeahbo, Norman Brown
and the Jones Benally Family
for seeing through my skin and into my heart.